To Touch Another

My Love, My Life, My Laughter

By
Shirley Hale

PublishAmerica
Baltimore

First printing

ISBN: 1-4137-7360-5
PUBLISHED BY PUBLISHAMERICA, LLLP
www.publishamerica.com
Baltimore

Printed in the United States of America

This book is dedicated to my family, all my friends, neighbors, acquaintances, co-workers, and all those who may have touched my life in one way or another over the years.
We gather so much from others, be it in minute amounts when we don't even realize it until a later time, or perhaps in bonus amounts when it hits us on the head like a hammer.
Regardless, we are different from that time on.

To: Donna Pettinger –
My Best Wishes to you dear. I hope you enjoy these pages from my heart.
Love from Mexico,
Shirl Sept. 6, 2005

"Love can come to you at any age.
It's not only for the young.
The older you are when it reaches you,
The younger you become."
Del

Acknowledgments

I'd like to thank the people who have, time and again, encouraged my writing over the years. Those who especially come to mind are:

~ my sister and her husband, Judy and Jerry Hackett
(you knew I could do this before I did);

~ my daughters, Holly McCaddin and Robin Hale,
and my son, Jeff Hale;

~ fellow poets at the Starlite Café
who offer so much encouragement;

~ and Michael James Cook,
the inspiration for most of my writing these days.

My Love

To Touch Another

The tree that grows so stately there
In leaves of green…soon to be bare
Such is life for all we know
Soon to come ~ the glistening snow
To cover all sins in the land
Erase the errors of the hand
Seemingly to make anew
To greet in spring the skies of blue
'Tis bad we can't do this as well
For none to see and none to tell
But once we touch another person
He is touched and that's for certain
No taking back…no snow to cover
No erasing of your lover
The heart still breaks, falls to the ground
And by the wind it's blown around
No Winters day can make it right
No snow to hide it from your sight
The coldness though is of this season
We all suffer for this reason
Yet, not to touch is not to live
For what is life with naught to give

Your Kiss

The first to touch each other
How soft and subtle the kiss.
Our lips tell much and oh, the touch
I remember nothing like this.
They're hot and wet, so very sweet
Heart racing, I can hardly keep
My wits about me ~ kiss me again.
My bottom lip sucked softly in
Melting against you ~
Your lips trail downward,
Ever charging me within.
You nibble my ear ~ taste my neck.
Your lips searing as they touch.
I'll never ~ ever get enough.

My One and Only, My First Love

My yesterdays have all but died,
I've lost my one and only love.
I cannot run ~ nor can I hide
For him I am a mourning dove.

The days drag on and turn to years
Forever changed ~ I dream of him.
I care not, but life remains
Need him close to breathe him in.

This loneliness is such a curse
My empty heart ~ his softest kiss
I thank God that he went first ~
I'd not want him to suffer this.

Someday we'll meet in heaven above
My one and only ~ my first love.

I Keep You Near

Your voice drifts softly in my mind
~ you whisper in my ear.
A feeling washes over me
~ as if you're really here.
Your lips light gently on my lips
~ and linger on my breasts.
Hands trace hot patterns on my hips
~ my mind awaits the rest.
Your arms draw me ever closer
~ skin hot and wet as dew.
Breathing the same air together
~ I am one with you.
My mind helps me to keep you near
~ and hold you in my heart.
Our souls are intertwined
~ and never more shall part.

Because of a Man

Just when I think I've settled in,
you make me feel like sixteen again.
My spirits simply seem to soar
higher and higher than ever before.
I thank God for you with nightly prayer
and ask that He keep you in His care.
You've brought so much life and love to me
forever grateful ~ I will always be.
I want you to know that you have my heart
It's here for you and will never part.
The future may hold so much for us,
we need only share our love and trust.
I still find it hard to understand
how I go from sixty to sixteen ~
because of a man.

A Gentle Man

A gentle man I went to see ~
Oh, he was so kind to me.
He took me to see many a sight,
And cared for me with such delight.

We boated along the rocky coast,
And in the morning, we shared toast.
We laughed, we cried, we snuggled up~
He's my darling buttercup.

We toured the coast, the shops and beach,
Walked in the ocean in our bare feet.
We picked up rocks and steadied each other
As we trekked through the sands together.

On Sunday morning he took me to pray
For this is the day I was to be saved.
He showed me high mountains with many trees.
We ran through a warm rain in the breeze.

What more could I ask from this gentle man,
Who has given so much from his heart and his hand.
He'll ever hold on to a piece of my heart ~
I always knew that, right from the start.

Take Me There

Take me to that special place somewhere...

Out there in space
Looking in your eyes so blue
I am drifting off with you
Leaving this world way behind
Going someplace far more kind
A kiss falls gently as a leaf
Senses heightened...

Beyond belief
Soft, moist lips

Hands caressing
Barely aware that we're undressing
A waft of you fills my being
Our minds together ever seeing
Floating there alone with you
Loving all the things you do
Spending all my days that be
In this special place with thee
Take me there

As we begin...
To free the silence from within

This Man in My Life

So far away in distance
Yet ~ so close at heart
Longing seems to overcome me
Almost from the start

Every day we touch our lives
With letters all in type
The words just flow so easily
Telling of our plight

Taking each day as it comes
Hoping for the best
To touch each other as before
And tell each other ~ yes

We're so much more than lovers
We are deep-down friends
Understanding what's inside
Not knowing what's 'round the bend

This is life ~ it changes so
We must go where led
Sharing our love with one another
Keeping God ~ in heart and head

Jacob

His eyes of blue look into mine
Blond curls surround his head
I'd love to hold him all the time
And share with him my bed

We're so close to one another
A million kisses I could give
He would return them one by one
If it took all that he lived

Such devotion I've not seen
Nor shall I ever see again
He teases me and plays with me
So much ~ I see in him

Not one will share my feelings
Not one will know my heart
I've had so many dealings
With this guy from the start

We'll both always remember
How we tease and then make up
He'll be two ~ this November
My darling grandson, Jacob

The Touch of My Lover

How tempting is the thought of me
Being there alone with thee ~
Caring not the time nor weather
Laying my head on pillows of feather
Silk'n sheets and candles all glowing
A breeze through the window ~
curtains flowing
Feeling our bodies touching each other
Knowing what's coming…
the touch of my lover
Send me to places I've never been
Give me that special feeling within
Wanting to give you more that I get
As my body is hot ~ and so very wet
You must give me lessons
so that I may be…
All that you have become to me

Sweet Times

Sweet times ~ I recall with no trouble at all
Times spent with you ~ when we had such a ball
You made me laugh so hard ~ I would cry
I couldn't stop, no matter how hard I'd try
My tummy would hurt, I'd get a pain in my side
I'd cover my mouth ~ my head I would hide
No one has ever affected me in this way
We shared something special every day
I need that again ~ need to feel close
Need those sweet times, I miss them the most
We understood each other without making a sound
Just needed one another ~ no one else around
We shared so much ~ ever since we were kids
Help me find another ~ to do what you did

Reality Sets In

The unmistakable distant ocean
Casts a faceless peace onto time.
Comfort my desire…
As my search is empty.
I'll hunger for love…
Knowing my day will never be,
This truly saddens me.

Gone

Accept death…
For unspoken grief
Is sorrow's voice concealed
Absence of touch
Gone…
Like a stolen belief
Time hidden in eternity

The Lovers' Dance

His presence towers over her as candles softly glow
He is here to give to her ~
All he can bestow.
He sought her out to pleasure her, of this she is aware.
She trembles with anticipation
Of all he's going to share.
The shadow of her lover is cast upon her soul.
His body ~ lean and long and bare ~
Glistens ~ head to toe.
She turns not away from him for he hath cast his spell.
She is here to ride the storm
And never more to tell…
Slowly he disrobes her as she stares into his eyes.
She can't take her gaze from him
She is mesmerized.
This dance of lovers has begun slowly with first touch,
His feathered fingers ~ how they linger
She loves all this so much.
His kiss is of the mist that touches all of time.
It lingers there ~ just barely there,
Then moves on down the line.
Her clothes are all discarded now ~ strewn upon the floor
She cares not, but just for him,
As she cries out for more.
His skin is hot against hers, they set their world aflame.
She whimpers and she moans,
As she calls out his name.

This dance is not for all you see ~ just a special lover,
He has to understand and be
Unlike any other.
Their fate is sealed forever on this lovers' bed.
The bond is made ~ the dance begun, and
Lives on in her head.

love IS blind

I'm filled with emotions you left behind
how do I cleanse myself
and start anew?
Torturing myself each and every day
reliving the memories of
you ~ You ~ YOU!
Should I look differently at the time we shared
and just be thankful
for our time together?
I wish I could
~ but I can't ~
I am scared.
You stirred up emotions and feelings forever.
It was light-hearted stuff for you,
now I'm sure.
For me it went deep to my soul.
How could I be so far off track?
When will I ever be whole?
I try to move on ~
to put you behind…
keep myself busy
with so much to do,
but you simply refuse
to stay out of my mind.
Will I ever be rid of you?
I even try to hate you ~
feel sorry for you…

see you for what you really are!
Then I drift back to the bed that we shared
and see I haven't come very far.
Maybe some day I'll look back and laugh
wondering why
I wasted my time…
over a guy who thinks he's so wonderful.
I should have seen it even if I were blind!

Michael

(dedicated to my grandson who was killed one week after his 15th Birthday by a driver under the influence of drugs)

We gather strength from years gone by
as we sift through the photos
~ talking of good times
~ reliving the memories
and preparing our final goodbye

Our tears are not for you, but for ourselves
as we will be missing you so…
it's hard to let go
even knowing
we'll be reunited one day

You and Grandpa will have to help us
~ help us to be strong
~ and to continue on
We long to hold you one more time
to kiss your cheek…
to stop the time

The fish'n's good way up there ~
So, you and Grandpa have some fun
We know he has been waiting for you
His fishing buddy ~ his grandson

We Wait

two souls lost in life's storm
longing for what might have been

the dance ~
no longer within reach
empty arms left longing to hold

your touch ~
but a mere dream in time

your kiss ~
so long awaited,
now lost

the memories we almost shared
moments so precious to both

and yet ~
we wait once more

Winds of Love

to wonder and dream the night away
even ponder ~
throughout the day
your face, your stature,
and your stance ~
will we be friends without romance
or
will the winds of love blow through
giving us our worldly due
filling hearts
with love and laughter
comfort us with what we're after
we take the chance ~
we cannot lose
we've only two that we can choose
to be best friends ~
as we grow old
or
to be true loves to have and hold

A Blanket of Sadness

The fog settles in…
forming a thick blanket of sadness around me,
I welcome its protection.
The softness of the rain soothes my tired soul.
It slowly cleanses me of the pain…
the pain I refused to face.
The clouds reflect my innermost feelings…
they hide me from my emotions.
I will wallow in this day and this night.
I will rise again to a new dawn…
and a new day tomorrow
~ free.
Free of an addiction that has held me for months.
It had to be ~ he had to go…
I knew it in my gut.
I thought him strong ~ but I was wrong.
He was too weak to be honest.
Honesty ~ is all I ask.

A Place to Hide

Soft feelings settle over me as my mind drifts off to you
thinking of the things we talk ~
and all that we may do
These feelings washing through my being take me far away
from this world ~ as I know it
each and every day
I like this newfound place ~ a place where I can hide
sometimes I cuddle up in there
pretending I've not cried
I bring you with me to this place where we can be together
just you and me, our thoughts that be
all alone forever
We get to know each other ~ the soul is there to touch
starting slowly as we begin,
not knowing very much
As we settle into one another, feelings start to grow
the rhythm of hearts beating…
the candles all aglow
Soft music from the background seems to disappear…
As sighs and moans replace it
for all the world to hear
I'd rather stay here with you ~ my lover at my side
than travel back from where I've come
with no place left to hide

Night's Shadows

Under the cloak of the darkness and shadows of night
I can let my hair down and my wings take flight
As I soar to the heavens and swoop down so low
I search for my lover…wherever I go

He's there, too, in night's shadows, he's searching for me
Longing for my lips and the caressing to be…
His face is still hidden, but familiar I'm sure
The scent of his body is my beckoning lure

As we melt into darkness and know one another
No words need be spoken…just take of your lover
Time will stand still as two souls become one
Then a new day will dawn along with the sun

The Melding

My emotions ebb and wane, the tears fall as rain
oft times his words find me ~
in loneliness and sorrow.
He seduces me with these words,
seeking out my smiles
lifting up my heart and touching my innermost soul.

Connected only by this cyberspace of words,
no faces,
learning so much of each other…
from each other.
Man should learn of the total honesty within before
judging is made by mere surface vision.

He is more known to me…this one is trustworthy,
it's as though we befriended each other as children.
We've grown together forming a bond of total friendship,
trust, openness, understanding, love and hope.

No promises are made…no binding ties formed,
our presence is a gift to one another…
delivered out of desire,
given of free will…
accepted with joy,
never taken for granted…
excitedly anticipated,
and always appreciated.

The Sea

The swelling of the surf, the lovely melody it plays
Cymbals crash as the waves pound on heavy sand
I've danced to this music in days gone before ~
In the innocence of my young adulthood ~

~ with my only true love ~
~ he knows who he is ~

He introduced me to this enchanting land of surf and sea
In fact, he introduced me to all things that be

~ he cared for me ~
~ and I for he ~
'til death do us part

So, here I am…standing on life's secluded beach
so alone ~ so free
Yet tied to a memory so burned into my being
That the ocean brings him ever close to me once more
Breathing in the salt air ~ watching the rhythm of the sea
Hearing his whispers in my ear ~ feeling the music
Reliving the power of our love on moonlit sands,
~ my captain, my love ~

Desires of a Woman

One conjures up the images of the perfect man
He must be six feet tall ~ and tan
She can dream and add on all kinds of things
Must be totally unattached, without any strings
She must be number one at the top of his list
He must totally love to kiss and be kissed
He'll never leave her emotions to chance
He must not drink, but love to dance
He'll make love in the morn or afternoon
And he'll make love in any room ~
Caring not the time of day
He'll also do it in any way
He's quite inventive, you must know
Always willing and ready to go ~
To the ends of the earth for her every day
And he's full of fun and likes to play
He has hair on his chest for her fingers to twist
And sensuous lips awaiting her kiss
He's so loving and gentle, she'll be begging for more
Then he's more demanding and she is his whore ~
Their desire stays lit by the games that they play
So totally matched for a romp in the hay ~
She'll sprinkle her kisses from his head to his toes
He'll not forget her ~ wherever he goes

A Sensuous Lure

As I enter my room and close the door
I'm letting my clothes fall to the floor
Need to rid my body of this day
Need to relax in every way
The shower beckons me to its stream
As I inhale vapors feeling the steam
Oh ~ when that water first touches my skin
It's rinsing away my troubles and sin
My tension is running right down the drain
My muscles no longer hold any pain
As I lather up with scents smelling so sweet
I look down and notice my feet
Soap bubbles swirling around my toes
As around and around the water goes
Thinking of things that have been ~
Wishing my lover could join me again
Sensual memories remain in this bath
I can't shower without bringing them back
It was truly a night unlike any other
As I lathered up the skin of my lover
The Oil of Olay was appropriately named
No wonder it's so well known and famed
Such fun we had with all that we did
So many senses that we un-hid
Pleasure can be so simple and pure
This shower holds such a sensuous lure

I Bed Down with Thee

The urgency of the kiss and the touching of our skin ~
the air between us so heated up,
we hurriedly begin
Not knowing if we'd have again ~ this special time together
and just knowing this may be
the last time ~ forever
The gentleness of your stroke and the power of your kisses
lead me to believe
you'll answer all my wishes
Your fingertips, your tongue,
the whispered words across my skin
all touch me in so many ways
I beg you to come in
Just when I think our energies are totally all spent ~
the man in you once again
comes back from where it went
Not one could ask for any more than what you've given me
I count my blessings every time
I bed down with thee ~

Slip Under the Covers

Slip under the covers and find me there
Touch under my nightie ~ anywhere
Enter my mind, my body, my soul
Take of me and make me whole

Slip under the covers and kiss me there
Touch deep in my heart ~ anywhere
Enter me softly, so subtle, so true
Take me away ~ away with you

Slip under the covers and breathe of me
Touch my very being, and within thee
Enter me everlasting, leave nevermore
Take of the one ~ you solely adore

I Dream You

I would take you into me ~ soft touch upon my skin
you would soothe my longing,
my heated desire within

I feel your hot breath upon me ~ even as I sleep
I dream your kisses come to me…
so soft, so wet, so sweet

Your hands explore my body as my mind takes me away
I breathe your essence deep within
so happy for this day

We are so in tune to one another ~ time is standing still
I am at your beck and call,
do with me what you will

I should dream you always ~ if this keeps you nearer me
We need to touch each other…
embrace so tenderly

The Sweeter the Tune

I see you lying there ~ covers cast upon the floor
Shimmering in the candle light
as I turn to lock the door
Your scent surrounds me ~
as I breathe you in
Setting the mood for what's to begin
I've dreamed of this night ~
all is sublime
Being with you…taking our time
Exploring each other ~
hands, fingers and tongues
Who knew we could have this much fun
Our bodies so in tune ~
each to the other
Giving all one can, then take of your lover
Curtains dancing to and fro
lit up by the moon
And now you know
The older the fiddle ~ the sweeter the tune

Stirrings from Within

Come to me as before, my love ~ tenderness of touch
enveloped in thy aura,
wanting thee so much
stirrings from within…
knowing you enter unto me
I ask not how but take thee in ~
can this really be

Take me as before, my love ~ as the time stands still
intensity is heightened,
I am at thy will
stirrings from within…
going far back in time
I ask not how or why ~
know that I am thine

I beg ye come to me ~ a hundred times no less
surrounded by a waft of thee,
held in thy tenderness
I plead ye never leave this eve…
lest that I should die
take me with thee please, my love ~
else I stay to cry

Love Still Lives

For thou hast cast me away,
Far away from thee.
My love still lives within
In spite of what may be.
My tears fall silent in the night;
No one to kiss them gone.
Comfort is not found nearby…
Loneliness fades with dawn.
'Tis hollowness that fills my heart,
how did this come to be?
Was I not seeing what was there,
only what I wished to see?

Sea Shells

As a young girl I walked alone on the beach
I picked up the shells…all within reach.
Some I'd toss back to the sea as they are,
Others I'd take home and keep in a jar.
Always taken by their colors, their sizes and shades,
How'd God come up with all the things that He made?

As I matured and still walked along on that sand
With my true love…us both holding hands.
I'd look into his eyes and see so much love…
I was sure God sent him to me from above,
Always taken by his humor, his passion, his lips.
How'd God come up with all the things that He did?

I'm walking alone now on life's lonely beach.
The magical things are far out of my reach.
The shells still show beauty and colors so bright…
Sea grasses are swaying and birds still in flight,
Always taken by salt air and all the sea gives.
How come God took him ~ and left me to live?

December

She's waiting for him as he enters the room,
he's so handsome and tall and strong.
They kiss softly at first…then with more passion,
it seems like it's been so long.

His shoulders are broad and his muscles so hard,
did she forget the feel of his skin…
His hands roam down her back and hips,
he is raising that feeling within.

The spell evolves as they begin to undress,
stealing kisses and touching each other.
The light is turned out leaving only the glow
of the candle and a glimpse of your lover.

They take of the other not more than they give…
the night seems to go on everlasting.
Not an inch of the bed that didn't give in
nor a space on a body was fasting.

She lay in his arms both totally spent…
this is a night they'll always remember.
As he kisses her eyelids, her cheeks and her lips…
They will always remember December.

Help Me, My Darling

So what if I never find someone to love me as you did
Will I remain in loneliness ~
have to keep my feelings hid
Must I paste this smile across my face and just go on pretending
Will my broken heart, my lonely nights ~
go on never ending
I don't think I can go through life so lonely, sad and blue
Help him find his way to me ~
I have to count on you
Make sure he has your humor, your loving ways, your style
He can have hair ~ or not,
but please let him have your smile
If he has your compassion and your light and tender touch
He would be so wonderful ~
am I asking way too much?
I'll leave this up to you, for you know me better than all
He need not be too handsome,
but it'd be nice if he were tall
I'll just go about my daily tasks ~ I know you have a plan
Just give me a hint when he gets here,
so I can take him by the hand

Never-ending Ecstasy

Let me drink of you…
pour your sweetness over me
bathe me in your love
drown me in your sea

Let me enter you…
our souls meld into one
the tide rolls in ~
the waters rise…
we are the setting sun

Let the waves wash over us…
as we lay upon the shore
in never-ending ecstasy
lovers ~ evermore

Are You Trying to Say Goodbye

Do I hear words that aren't spoken
Do I read between the lines..
Are you trying to say goodbye
And pretending all is fine

True love can conquer everything
The tallest mountains, the raging sea
You must want it more than life itself
You have to want it…like me

Let's put things in perspective
Speak what's in your heart
I must know where you stand
I don't want to see us part

How often does one find true love
In these our final years…
Cherish what we've found together
Don't make me shed your tears

So take your time ~ think it over
We have so much to give
We owe it to each other…
We've but one life to live

My Last Breath

If my days were all numbered
and I had but one to live…
I'd spend that day
with you, dear,
sharing all I have
to give.

My kisses I would squander
on your body
head to toe…
I'd leave a spot
not untouched,
because
I love you so.

My hands would leave caresses
with their gentle,
loving touch…
I'd leave that memory
with you,
as I'm loving you
so much.

With my last dying
breath…
I'd breathe you
into me,

I'd have always
that part
of you..
wherever
I may be.

I'll Be There

I'll be that special thought
that comes from within
The whispered breeze ~
in the sound of the wind
I'll be the aroma of coffee..
the very first cup
The one savored the most
when you wake up
I'll be the snap of the twig
under foot as you walk
The hesitation in voice ~
when starting to talk
I'll be the song of the bird
soaring over the land
The sound of the ocean ~
washing up on the sand
I'll be the dream unremembered
upon your first waking
The beginning of each and every
breath you are taking

I Drink of Him

A glass of wine my lips recall,
the taste of his
my love…
of all.
Another sip I drink of him,
his breath is
buried deep
within.
The goblet tips up
one more time…
he's flooding back
into my
mind.
I'll not survive alone
again…
without the wine
or without
him.

Torn

Emotions running high
all pent up here
within ~
Should I let go,
say farewell…
to live in pain
again?
Seek I not
another's man…
for he surely
must be
true.
Dare I not
another time…
bid him fond
adieu.

Guardian Angel

Envelop me in your unseen wings,
ever safe, reassured and consoled.
May I feel your presence…
evermore ~
let my life to you unfold.
You lead the way ~ I will follow…
take my hand,
else I shall stray.
The journey is long and slow and hard,
your comfort will guide my way.
As time passes and troubles fade,
you'll lift me gently upon your wings
We'll soar up to the heavens ~
swoop down to the ocean
to see what the rest of life brings.

Secrets from Within

I'll leave not
In misery.
My soul
Shall not depart.
Desire will remain…
In my
Unburdened heart.

When all
Is then revealed
~ Secrets from Within ~
I'll ever dream
You near…
Where you
Have always been.

Sweet Depths Within

As he looks deeply into my eyes
I'm spellbound and hypnotized
Soft hand placed upon my cheek
My will is his, as legs go weak
Tenderly he kissed my lips
Sending vibrations to my wanting hips
Ecstasy now fills my head
As he now lowers me into his bed

The sheets so cool against my skin
I draw a breath and take him in
A pillow placed beneath my head
So softly on this featherbed
From somewhere comes a distant song
I eye his body ~ lean and long
Walls adorned in candles glow
Awaiting the upcoming show

My breath so quickened with his touch
I've never wanted one so much
He took my body ~ he took me slow
Knowing just where his tongue should go
His hands, his lips, his fingertips…
Kept pace with the rhythm of my hips
Then sinking to sweet depths within
At last we drift to Earth again

The Breeze of Love

You enter on the breeze of the early morn
Curtains flowing open to let you pass
Gently you caress my body ~
Ever so gently you whisper upon my bare skin
Your fragrance I find enticing…intoxicating
Envisioning in my mind behind closed eyes..
The being I so desire ~ the one I so need
One who will transport me from this oneness
Let me go with you ~ take me into your stream
Let me fly with you as you rustle the leaves
As the trees bow down to you
May I feel the sunshine as you do
Endure the raindrops and the thunder
Hold me ever close in your care
Leave me not alone to never know you again

For What

others look to me ~ for what
oft times I wonder…for I have no control
life meanders by, slipping into the past
unfulfilled dreams linger and fade to darkness
I grab for the prize…look to my hand
it remains empty, as is my heart
this elusive part of my life
my future this must be ~ insecurity reigns within
to be rescued from this…ha ~ surely you joke
this time is not long, yet saturated with loneliness
sopping up the tears hidden deep in my soul
trudging ever forward toward nothingness
reaching out to grasp the end ~
the end of the rope that is invisible to my eyes
oh how I dread these mornings
to start anew ~ for what

My Fragile Heart

My imagination is running
With the wind
I can't seem to keep a hold
On my emotions
They roam freely in the breeze ~
Unable to gather them…
Remaining helpless and vulnerable
My heart is exposed,
Fragile…
Capable of being shattered
Into shards
Ever piercing my soul
Leaving me bleeding…
Feelings flowing
Freely ~
Mixing with
My salt-filled tears
To never dry
Forever
More

The Mere Thought of You

If I could touch my hand to yours far across the miles,
my heart would pound, my soul would sing…
I'd be so full of smiles.

Even the mere thought of you…your lips, your eyes, your hair,
is almost too much for me…
more than I can bare.

Your voice has left no echo, not a sound for me to hear
I can but imagine…
how loving and sincere.

Your eyes…I know they sparkle
showing love and tenderness.

Your lips ~
oh, how I long for them,
and your most passionate kiss.

Your hair ~
I'd run my fingers through
and breathe it deep within.

This longing stored within my soul where it has always been,
'tis waiting here for you, my love, yours only…for the taking.
My every moment is of you, while asleep or in my waking.

Love Has Entered

Surely time had passed me by,
As tears flowed down onto these keys.
Seeking love ~ yet left to cry,
Until the day you called for me.

Enter me and make me whole,
Take of me ~ what I can give.
Take my body…take my soul,
Be at my side…all that I live.

Two souls bonding ~ being one,
Love has entered us at last…
All the future still to come,
As we move forward from the past.

So Near to You

So near to you…
and yet so far.
these keys take me
to where you are.
My heart remains inside of me…
though every inch
is full of thee.

I dream your lips
to kiss on mine,
as I touch upon
your face so kind.
I take your breath into me deep,
each night as I
drift off to sleep.

Every morn when I awake,
every moment of time
you take.
You fill my soul
with dreams of love.
You're Heavensent
from up above.

My Sugar Kiss

As I dream of you…and what's to be
I only hope you dream of me
Time passes slowly in the night
With you so far from my sight

Do you yearn for me…
My skin so fair
The softest scent
Of my hair

My nipples…
Standing up for you
My tongue ~
and all that it can do

My kisses strewn
across your chest
My little licks
on all the rest

My fingertips upon your lips
The way I straddle
Both your hips

The dirty talk…
My cries and moans
Thc way I rattle
All your bones

Do you long
For all of this???
Mmmmmmmm, so do I,
My Sugar Kiss xxxxx

My Invisible Visit

As you sit in your chair with your bathrobe on
I'm invisible to you…
as I move along
You lay back in your chair with feet propped up
In your hand is your coffee ~
black, in a cup
You sip ~ resting your head back on the chair
Oblivious to the fact ~
that I'm even there
I like it this way for I can look at you
Stand back…
and see all that you do
Tweety is there ~ right down by your side
She sees me
with her eyes open so wide
Her tail is a wagging, but you pay her no mind
Just pat her on the head
and rub her behind
I see the socks that you wear to warm up your feet
And the loving looks
that come from dear Tweet
Kissy Boy is taking his mid-morning snooze
As I take all this in,
I'm getting the blues
I bend down to kiss you there in your chair
Right on your head ~
where you used to have hair

You're such a darling…and I smile as I see
On the table beside you ~
is a poem from me

As Together We Will Be

How far can our love travel ~ from sea to shining sea
The feelings that we share, I'm sure we're meant to be
I listen to the thunder as the rain comes pouring down
Breathing in the air ~ wishing you'd come 'round

The beating of our hearts ~ continue on as one
As you have my afternoon, I see your setting sun
The clouds way over head...you sent straight to me
I see your art in them ~ it's ever-changing scenery

Someday we'll share the ocean, be it yours or perhaps mine
We'll be walking hand in hand ~ through the rest of time
Our clouds and sun will be the same, we will surely see
It matters not where we are ~ as together we will be

This Bottle of White Zin

I unlock that secret place where I keep you deep within
Only after that bottle empties of most of the white zin
The mood should be relaxed as your memories flood to mind
Taking me way back to you ~ far back there in time

It's as if you're still here with me, as if I never cry
I see you and I breathe of you ~ just like you didn't die
I must do this just for me, so I don't go insane
When I don't, I can't go on ~ I suffer too much pain

I try to listen for your voice ~ whispering words to me
I long to feel your touch, and to put my hands on thee
A kiss ~ just one more kiss ~ lingering on my lonely lips
Your hands caressing me ~ my breasts and then my hips

If only we could make love one more time together
I'd hold this picture in my mind always and forever
For now I live on old memories I have stored within
And drown my sorrows in my tears and…
This bottle of white zin

Our Lovers' Bed

I see you standing there, a special look is in your eyes
Remembering from the past ~ I am mesmerized
We begin undressing, as the room is filled with heat
Our breathing quickens...hearts speed up the beat

As our bare bodies touch, it's more than we can stand
We lie down beside each other as you gently kiss my hand
The sheets are cool against our skin, as we take our time
Your hands around my head ~ your lips devouring mine

As we create new memories amid the moans and sighs
Soft guitar music in the background brings back days gone by
Your lips search out secret places...only known to you
Our hands find ones so familiar, as we start anew

I've dreamed of this night for so long ~ a memory it seems
You're taking me to new heights known only in my dreams
Your hot breath covering me ~ I see the burning in your eyes
I feel your hard and glistening body...the strength within your thighs

The candle burns down slowly as we bask within its glow
Time has no more meaning ~ as we love each other so
This endless night turns into dawn...a sky aglow in red
May we always feel as we do now, in this, our lovers' bed

Picture

As I see you on my night stand
You always look the same
Done black and white
In that natural frame

As I trace around your lips
I can swallow and I taste
The passion of your kisses
All about my face

As I look into your eyes
I want so to see
The desire residing there
As I have for thee

I want to whisper in your ears
To kiss upon your head
To give you all I have
As we share a lovers' bed

Touch of the Sand

I can wish you near me…right here by my side
I seem to hear your voice
Arriving on the tide

Your touch caresses me all 'round…carried on the wind
Giant waves wash over me
To take away my sin

I draw my heart for you…right here in this sand
For we shall never walk
Together
Hand in hand

My heart has washed away…taken by the sea
As you walk along your shore
Touch of the Sand
~ And me ~

Distance

All I'll ever do…is know you from afar
We share the moon and sun
Look at the same stars

Heartbeats fill my chest, resounding off to you
Riding on the tide
Across the ocean blue

The white caps are my kisses, lapping at your shore
My hugs, the little shells
That wash up by your door

My dreams fly with the seabirds, swooping down to see
As I dream of you…
If you also dream of me

After the Lights Go Out

After the lights go out
Your words dance before my eyes
I begin to feel your presence
I start to hear your sighs

After the lights go out
There's loneliness in my heart
I'm imagining your touch
As the tears begin to start

After the lights go out
My mind brings you back to me
For you'll remain here in my heart
Right where you should be
~ After the Lights Go Out ~

True Confession

My heart's an open door
Bring me from the blue
Seeking words of kindness
Again it waits for you
Believe me so completely
This is my concession
Written on my heart
Words of true confession

You and I

Whisper to me softly,
Telling of your love
Let me hear those words
Only we two share
Your soft voice resonates
Deeply within
I adore you so, my love ~
Do I dare?
There'll be no regrets,
For we live in each other
Bonded by words
Written on our hearts
Created within our souls…
Breathed into one another
With truth and understanding
For what we share
Is found by yet so few
Seldom so deep and profound ~
We are truly blessed
You and I

Moments Unequaled

The night is sultry and so is the mood
As desire is aroused within
I can hardly believe we're together at last
Our love about to begin

I wear my red teddy just for you
For I know what fills your desire
Come join me on this feather bed
For a heated night of fire

A kiss on your eyelids, then on your lips
I breathe in the scent of you
Your hands roaming all over me
I am loving all that you do

You toy with the straps of my teddy
As it drops down around my waist
My body half exposed to you
As you begin to taste

A gentle breeze drifts through the room
And touches upon our skin
We barely notice the waft of air
But for the smell of jasmine

We touch, we taste, we can't get enough
Of love's eternal pleasure

Every nerve is heightened
The momentum building
Moments we'll always treasure

From deep within our fountains spew forth
To bathe us in each other
Knowing no other feelings shared
Could ever equal these
With your lover

Summer's Night of Thunder

Thunder rolls across the darkened sky
This evening is hot, sultry, and steamy
We inhale the humidity in the air
Disrobe…feel the gentle breeze
Upon our dampened skin
Let the wind gently whisper
Its softness all around us
For this is nature
At its best…
A bolt of lightening
Streaks the darkness
Illuminating the paleness of our skin
Showing so pure in nature's storm
A scent of honeysuckle
Gentle thunder becomes
But a distant murmur
Traveling through time and distance
Leaving us to ourselves
And the tiny raindrops
Dancing on our bodies
Washing away our final inhibitions
As we fulfill nature's call
Within

My Star of Love

As I sit here by my window
Gazing at the stars above
A bright star shone upon me
Could this be my star of love?
As I stared into its brilliance
My mind wandered back in time
To another world, another place
Where love was so sublime

It seems so long ago…
Since I've felt him close to me
I dream of him, I taste of him
Only pictures ~ left to see
It seems another life…
One which I left behind
When days were filled with laughter
And love was far more kind

This star of love at which I gaze
Has touched upon my soul
I know his spirit lives within
And helps to make me whole
So if you see a star so bright
Twinkling in the dark
It simply is my lover
Sending a message to my heart

Phantom Lover

Alas, my love has come to me
As whispers on the wind…
I've awaited him so long
So lonely I have been

He lifts my heart to heaven
As I'm cradled in his arms…
Ever breathing in his scent
He gives me all his charms

My slightest wish is his command
Forever may he stay ~
My Phantom Prince, he may be
But I'll love him every day

We'll sail forever on the seas
As with the tide we flow ~
I will always bring him near
When I desire so

I bid farewell, my phantom lover
as you're wisped away to sea
I care not at your parting..
for I'll bring you back to me

My Fantasy

~ Mind ~
please bring to me
My Fantasy
let him be ~ everything to me
he may be short
or he could be tall
have lots of hair ~ or none at all
he'll be a good lover
with his gyrating hips
he'll seduce me ~ with his sensuous lips
a nice deep voice
so sexy and pure
he will then be ~ my loneliness cure
he must love to laugh
and like to have fun
for he will become ~ my honeybun
he'll come to me
each night in my bed
when I dream him up ~ here in my head

I Want Out

What if I did that which is out of place
Would that be so bad
Would I lose face

Who must I answer to today
Where should I turn
What will I pay

Can't I just live my life for me at last
Do as I wish
Forgetting the past

Would it be so bad if I just up and went
Took off on my own
I don't need consent

I feel so trapped living alone as I do
Yearning for more
Longing for you

A Change of Heart

A change of heart
Feelings so sure
Mine run so deeply
Mine run so pure
It's held by one
Whose words of
Forever
Reside in my soul
Leaving me
Never
The coin
Will not fall
To the ocean floor
It's held in my heart
Forevermore

Our Love

I cradle your head against my breast
Soothing your cares away
Your eyes close softly as I toy with your hair
Thanking God…for this day

Your breathing slows listening to my heart
Knowing the love held inside
We are so blessed to have found one another
Our love washing in on the tide

We both heard the sound of the Atlantic roar
Like a magnet it pulled us together
Our words mingling as did our hearts
With the sand and water forever

Death of the Heart

Love's words ~ spoken ~ play on one's heart
Spirits soar…to fall once more
Take of the soul ~ weakens one
Only dare, tread lightly there
The body lives…it does not part
So hard to bare ~ death of the heart

Talk to Me, Baby

Talk to me, baby ~ sing me the blues
Tell me you miss me and what you will do
Take away my loneliness…make me feel good
Do all the things you told me you would

Talk to me, baby ~ whisper in my ear
Tell me those words you know I love to hear
Make new memories for us to share
Tell of your love and how much you care

Talk to me, baby ~ with moans and with sighs
Tell me you love my breasts and my thighs
Take of our passion, our love, and our lust
Take all of me for I know that you must

Talk to me, baby ~ as you take me to the top
Tell me what I want and never, ever stop
You know what I love, you know my desires
I'm in need of your lovin' to put out these fires

Memories in the Dark

Memories in the dark, come by me to stay
Touch upon my cheek and dry my tears away
Whisper in my ear your words of tenderness
Caress upon my body…passions of your kiss
Hold me to you tightly as I breathe you into me
Memories in the dark…at last, now I can see

Inside

~ Inside ~
Things are not right…
I'm working on me
Into the night
No understanding,
Sadness invades
It's what I deserve
What I have made

~ Inside ~
I'm numb
I'll not be the same
No forgiveness for me
Not…from within
My heart is aware
Of what I've caused
My brain doesn't care
My life is on pause

~ Inside ~
I've a hole in my heart
My soul is weeping
Our love leaking out
Nothing for keeping
This is my life
I choose this for me
For I must live
In my misery

My Sweetest Rose

See through my eyes, there are no lies
Through these tears…I will survive
One is blind and cannot see
That of which can never be
Truth…no less, I promise you
My sweetest rose
Dripped with my dew
I wish you love…Deep within
Life anew ~ Soon to begin
Your dear heart filled with happiness
Your beautiful soul…Be always blessed

Good Morning!

As I awaken next to you,
My sleepy eyes take in the view
The rise and fall of your chest
As it rests against my breast
The rumbled hair upon your head…
The way you lay here in our bed
Whiskers…you almost grew
I simply love to look at you
My scarlet teddy's on the chair
Where it was tossed through the air
On a night ~ so wild as last
Two hours of sleep sure went fast
I touch my lips upon your eyes
As your hand goes to my thighs
I've a feeling we're not done
This morning's fun has just begun

I Feel Blessed

I feel this sadness in my heart
For all I've done from the start
Forgive me if you can, my dear
Hold me ever to you near

Never will I hurt again
Do not worry ~ no more pain
I've got to get my head on straight
Before it's just too damned late

You're the last I'd ever harm
A gentle man with all your charm
I feel blessed to have your love
Two souls joined from up above

He's the One

He takes me to him ~ for it matters not my time
Welcomes me into his heart
Can he be so blind?

I pledge my true love to him forever and a day
This comes from deep within
There's no more to say

His words touch inside my soul as no one has ever done
My heart drips with love
As if melted by the sun

I can't say enough about his kindness, love and tenderness
He's truly understanding
With him ~ I am so Blessed

Sharing Your Tears

The sound of the crickets and tree frogs
Is almost deafening ~
As darkness falls on this September eve
It's a sultry night…
No breeze to stir the air
I lay on these cool sheets and my thoughts
Turn to you, my love,
My angel, my sweetness
Wishing I could soothe you in your sorrow
Wanting to hold you to my breast
For comfort
Feeling the pain in your heart
Sharing your tears
A gentle waft of air moves the curtains
And crosses my body
I know it is sent from you
You know I am with you
Be at peace
Be safe
I love you always

To Follow My Heart

Searching, Seeking, Hoping to find
Something making sense in my mind
It's all old stuff ~ things of the past
Just how long does this stuff last?
I can't go on as I have been
Life was so much different then
That life for me, now is gone
Everything ~ has moved on
I've always been the predictable person
This was truly known for certain
Inside the box I'd surely stay
The same old thing, day after day
Always stayed within the lines…
Same old colors, time after time
Well, I've put my mind way up on the shelf
My heart's in charge of my new self
To follow my heart is what I'll do
This is so exciting and new
I'll fly with the wind
Unfurl my wings
Catch the updraft
Hear me sing!

My Life

Maryland

The scent of spring lingers in the air
~ fills me with feelings of little care
I love the nights as coolness invades
the waft of flowers comes in waves
Summer's heat is soon to come
sticky, humid, too much sun
kids all splashing in the pool
never thinking thoughts of school
nights are filled with tropical flair
not a breath stirs in the air
on dampened sheets I toss and turn
for central air ~ I do yearn
Then there's fall in all it's spender
no more colors could it render
crisp, cool nights ~ the harvest moon
long hay rides, so nice to swoon
Oh, winter's winds do blow too long
the land is barren ~ no birds for song
'til quiet snows cover the ground
only then shall its beauty be found
Time to start the cycle once more
every season has something in store
how lucky we are to have each one
no nicer place ~ under the sun

By the Bay

Just sitting here with my best friend
Here on this warm wooden dock
No cares, no worries, no phone
No kids, no work, no clock
My best friend ~ he'd rather concentrate
On the mallards swimming nearby
And snap at an occasional bee
My eyes close as I rest my head
Back on the rough, slivered piling
Sounds fill my head ~
The rumbling of an inboard
The rippling of a wake
The call of a blue heron
The lapping of water against old wood
Ah, yes ~ a waft of salt air fills my senses
So relaxing ~ so tranquil
I hear faint sounds of picnickers on the island
All is well ~
My best friend has now sprawled himself out
On the warm planks ~ sunning himself
As if to get a tan through all his golden fur
How peaceful life can be

Inside/Outside

Outside I hear the wind and rain
Inside I feel the deepest pain
A summer storm ~ the heat to break
As is my heart, 'tis tough to take
One would think that I'd move on
Leaving tears where they belong
Some days I seem to do so well
Others are a living hell
I pray to Him and lift my face
Ask Him to take me to His place
He helps me spend another day
In this world where I'm to stay
I gather strength ~ to spend another
Day on this earth without my lover
Inside I feel peace enter my heart
Outside the clouds ~ begin to part

I'm Your Grandma

I love you so dearly every day
I'm sorry for the things you have to say.
I'm just trying to raise you the best that I can
I'm your grandma and I try to plan

A future for you and also for Zach ~
Something to build on, so you can look back
And see that I've helped you in so many ways
I need no thanks ~ just peaceful days.

I don't need your back talk or words that are bad
You don't talk like that to Grandmom or Granddad.
You choose to take everything out on just me
All I want is respect, I hope you can see.

There's no need for the anger and acting so rude,
Shouting and screaming ~ you'll just sit and brood
You show no respect, I don't know what to do
I'm your grandma ~ I only wish I could help you.

Is it your MOM, with whom you should fight?
Perhaps this is so and she's not in your sight.
But here I am day in and day out
I'm your grandma ~ so go ahead and shout.

I don't know if I can take any more,
As I get older, I'd rather close this door.

Life would be so much better and easier to live
If you could move on and try to forgive.

Please try to love me ~ as I love you.
We've both lost your mom, not much we can do
To change things for us, we need be in prayer ~
Asking God to hold her and to take care.

My Friend

His golden hair
The forlorn stare
His eyes so brown
That little frown

He took my heart
Right from the start
Cute little toes ~
And cold, black nose

He's as loyal as can be
Always wants to be with me
Hates a bath, but loves to please
Got to kill those ticks and fleas

He's getting old, but so am I
Must hear him moan and sometimes cry
His painful hips, the stairs are slow
We stick together ~ I love him so

Her Operation

She did her best ~ tried to behave,
held back the tears, so very brave.
On her leg the doctor did write
his initials ~ right there in plain sight.

The nurses so helpful, loving and caring,
help her with everything ~ always sharing
little bits of information to her on her way,
to comfort and aid her throughout the day.

In about one hour, it should all be complete
the healing will begin ~ the goals set to meet.
Her eyes are still heavy, can't stay awake,
a sip of some liquid ~ "Is it daybreak?"

It's over, we tell her, she cannot believe
no memory ~ not an inkling ~ how can this be?
She sees the big bandage, the crutches and all,
time to go home and head down that hall.

To her bedroom ~ to comfort ~ to peacefully sleep
then wake up later for something to eat.
Family and friends ~ the visits will start
all make her feel better ~ all good for the heart.

Losing Him

In the autumn of my years
feeling empty ~ the future dim,
I've done nothing but shed tears.
Can't get over losing him.

My life forever changed that day.
Thanks be to God that I was near.
If only we knew, so we could say
our last goodbye ~ my darling dear.

I hold no anger, but the loss is great.
So many years of wedded bliss ~
Missing him so ~ I can hardly wait
'Til the day when again, I'll feel his kiss.

All Alone

Just me, myself, and I
That's all there is right here
The time I spend alone
Is usually quite dear

Sometimes I spend it in my room
Sitting in my easy chair
Sometimes I lay across the bed
To see my TV there

I close out all the goings-on
In and about the house
I like to have my quiet time
~ Quiet as a mouse ~

I savor these times more each day
Helps keep my mind clear
As I am getting up in age
And I hear the end is near

This is what the young ones say
I don't know if it is so
All I know is that I need my time
To be ~ All Alone

How Much Time

How much time do I have left?
I shouldn't really wonder
Whatever it turns out to be
I'll end up six feet under

I know that I am ready
all my ducks are in a row
When He calls me home
I'll be all set to go

I'd like you not to cry for me
you should already know
I long to join your father
who couldn't wait to go

I wanted to go with him
but had to wait my time
I had to raise these children
and listen to them whine

I told him not to leave me here
to raise them all alone
As soon as I get up to Heaven
with him I'll pick a bone

My life forever changed that day
as he left me here behind

I never thought I'd make it through
but everyone was kind

This loneliness just won't depart
and I'm tired of hanging in there
So don't cry a tear when I go Home
just be happy we're together

Feelings

The pain I feel is embedded down so deep
it's the pain of life and living and losing
mine never really goes away totally
it always lingers there to surface
~ Erupting ~
~ Boiling Over ~
~ Spewing Forth ~

To move on through open doorways
to rise up above all this doom
to feel that I could float above
to be lifted from this gloom
~ Rising ~
~ Floating ~
~ Drifting ~

Just to feel the burden begin to go away
to feel the weight be lightened
opening up my lungs for air
breathing a sigh of relief
~ Inhaling ~
~ Soothing ~
~ Relaxing ~

THIS WILL FADE IN TIME
AS IN TIME SHALL I

What If

What if ~ we had never met
and knew not of each other
What if ~ we had never kissed
never searching for a lover
What if ~ we were still alone
and our paths had never crossed
What if ~ you had chosen someone else
then I would still be lost

What if ~ time would just stand still
giving us our desire
What if ~ we could have time alone
again to light that fire
What if ~ both hadn't been so lonely
would we still have known that passion
What if ~ we can't recapture that
will it only be a has-been

What if ~ I treasure all our moments
matters not what comes my way
What if ~ I am ever thankful
for each and every day
What if ~ I never forget you
and all you've done for me
What if ~ I keep you in my heart
where you will always be

The Noise of Today

Oh, the music they play
So loud and pounding
Can't remember the day
That mine was that sounding

I can still hear my mom saying,
"You'd better turn that down!"
The record I was playing
Had such a great sound

There was Elvis or Fabian
And the Everly Brothers
The Beatles or Beach Boys
And the Brothers ~ Smothers

I played those records
'Til they were all shot
I knew all the words
And thought I was hot

Music today is driving me nuts
Volume always turned up so loud
Dancing around shaking boobs and butts
No more teens in this house, I've vowed

If Mom ever heard this stuff
She'd think mine was just great
She thought Sinatra was enough
Today's noise ~ she would hate

I'm So Thankful

So much fills my life ~ I must be ever thankful

My family is my life for me, and this may include you
You see there are four children and nine grandkids, too
Don't want to forget my kids' spouses, as they also count
There are many more at work ~ the number starts to mount

Then there is my church family ~ who have me in their care
And of course the aunts and uncles, who live just everywhere
Then don't forget my sisters ~ I wish that they were here
Thank God for my family, all of whom are dear

I can't forget my husband, who left me here behind
He was a very gentle man ~ and to everyone was kind
We were blessed to have each other, nearly forty years
Each day I miss him so ~ I still cry those tears

There is so much good in people, here and everywhere
We need only look inside and see just what's in there
I thank God for all I have and His blessings unto me
What will be in my life, I give thanks to Thee

This Time in My Life

It ain't easy getting old ~ and I know this well
Instead of working all day long
I need to sit a spell
My hair has gotten thinner ~ and oh, so gray
And I have gotten fatter
Afraid it's here to stay

I can't see as well ~ need to wear glasses
Which now have three lenses
No men will make passes
My fingernails don't grow so pretty and long
I no longer wear polish
What is going on!

No more high heels ~ they were my passion
I just wear the flat shoes
Care not about fashion
The car that I drive is "an old lady car"
It never gets washed
Nor driven too far

I seem to forget what each new day brings
Can't remember today
Only long-ago things
I'm in my own world ~ most of the time
Spending time alone
Or sometimes online

I guess it's my age ~ as my birthday draws near
Never thought I'd be this old
Guess I shouldn't fear
Suppose that I'll make it ~ as most seniors do
Not that I'll like it
But I'll tough it through

America

America the beautiful, you're still beautiful to me
We feel the pain, tears fall like rain
But our country still stands free
God bless those we lost and their loved ones, too
We feel the pain, tears fall like rain
But our country will pull through
The death and the destruction is way beyond belief
We feel the pain, tears fall like rain
We stand united in our grief
Not one heart has gone untouched by this horrendous act
We feel the pain, tears fall like rain
Our country will fight back
We are the home of the brave—land of the free
We feel the pain, tears fall like rain
We'll make it ~ they will see
Our flag is flying everywhere ~ all across our land
We feel the pain, tears fall like rain
As hand in hand we stand
So many prayers we do say and candles we do light
We feel the pain, tears fall like rain
As the daylight turned to night

God bless America ~ God bless us all

What Am I to Do?

Why am I here ~ what am I to do
I ask for His guidance to help make it through
I don't feel needed ~ like I used to be
Don't want to do much for myself, you see
These changes are hard to deal with in life
I want to give up, but know I must fight
I love my family so deeply and true
Why am I here ~ what am I to do

Saturday Mornings

Saturday ~ my favorite day of the week
I can turn over and go back to sleep
Waking up slowly as the sun shines bright
This is always my weekly plight
I turn on the TV ~ look for channel 11
This is my little part of heaven
Make my way to the coffee & start it to brew
Nothing much more in the kitchen to do
Back to my bedroom to open the curtains
Now comes the good time ~ of this I am certain
A fluff of the pillows to support my head
Now sitting, reading and drinking in bed
What could be better than this to do
As I guzzle down my best home brew
Only one thing better, is if my lover~
Were here with me, under the cover

Forever Changed

His spirit is within me
And will always be
I'm not whole without him
And will never be

Death rips out your heart
Life forever changed
Again I try to start
Never to…again

A Prayer for Strength

Oh, Lord, I'm feeling so alone I don't know what to do
This emptiness inside me just makes me feel so blue
I try to put the past behind and just look straight ahead
Some days are just so hard to take, I'd rather stay in bed

I drag myself to work each day and do my best while there
I put a smile upon my face, and try to fix my hair
Pretending that all is well, can only last so long
Then I come home to loneliness and everything's so wrong

Some days I just keep busy and pass the time that way
Then something triggers thoughts of him and there goes that day
Once on my mind, I miss him so, there's nothing left to do
After all these years, but cry more tears ~ I need help from You

Please give me strength to take each day as if he were still here
Although I know that he's with you, sometimes I feel him near
Try as I might to just go on ~ I'm having such a time
Please keep me on the straight and narrow and help me walk that line

My tears are not for him, but me ~ I just miss him so
I'll hold on here until the end, until it's time to go
When that day comes ~ You'll call me home and then
I'll be so happy to be with You ~ and see him again

Grandma's Soldier

It's hard to believe you're so far away
I'm happy for you and know you'll stay
To become an intricate part of a challenging team
Starting a new and exciting dream
You'll be serving our country ~ of this we are proud
When Basic is over ~ we'll shout very loud!
Though I'll not be there to help celebrate
To actually see you, I can hardly wait
Please know that my love is there with you
I bet you look cute in that uniform, too
It's hard to believe that my first grandchild
Is not running around and acting all wild
That she's struggling with PT, ammo and guns
And doing pushups ~ by the tons
That she's shooting a rifle
And doing guard duty
When I always thought of her
As my little cutie
I know when I see her, she'll stand tall and straight
She'll be her own person ~ she'll make my heart ache
I think of that baby ~ I held in my arms
Remember her first smile and all of her charms
Now she's all grown up and a soldier is she
How very proud ~ I am to be
Her grandma ~ with a grandchild so special
I LOVE YOU, Private. McCaddin, Katie L.

Such Is My Life

I hate my job ~ just can't go on
These kids make me insane
If I had my way, I'd stay in bed
Every hour, night and day
I find it hard to concentrate
And don't even care to try
Nothing seems important to me
And I don't know why ~
I'm feeling sad most of the time
And cry at the drop of a hat
I just hate being like this
But, this is where I'm at
The car broke down ~ the toilet, too
My vacuum doesn't suck
The oven won't cook the food
I guess I'm out of luck
My health is heading straight down hill
My aches and pains are many
I have more doctors than I have ills
I care not to see any
Such is my life ~ so I try to cope
With things as they come along
But I care not to deal with things
That's why everything's so wrong

If Only We Had Known

What can be done with a dilemma like this,
half of the time ~ these kids are so pissed.
They're nasty and care not what they say,
at times I think I'll not last through the day.
All that I ask is that we just live in peace,
respecting each other ~ all fighting must cease.
Be thoughtful of others, who may be asleep,
pay heed to the hours that we must keep.
If you can't speak words with more letters than four,
just keep your mouth shut ~ and say no more.
I must ask you to do a few things here and there,
Simply do them on time and please use some care.
I've asked you before to help cut down on the costs,
save water, electric and heating that's lost.
But do you care at all and listen to me?
Not on your life, 'til we lose it ~ you'll see.
Thank God you were young, forgetting the past,
where you lived in the slums, no food to last.
Roaches and rats slept with you there ~
our hearts ached for you and your care.
Grandpa and I didn't make your mom leave,
that is the last thing we wanted to see.
We tried to help all of you over the years,
your mom went and left us all in tears.
The liquor and drugs took her away ~
she loved you both, but chose not to stay.
Upon her return many weeks later,

she wanted you kids to take to a shelter.
We said, “No way…this cannot be done.”
So we went to court and felt that we had won.
Little did we know what we were in for,
from two of our grandkids whom we simply adored:
the hate and the lies, the fighting and screaming,
language that we find so demeaning.
Maybe you’d be better off ~ if you’d gone with your mother,
Out on the streets ~ not knowing what you’d suffer.
Not having a bed and a room to yourself,
not seeing doctors and dentists to better your health,
not having a home where your friends come to visit,
not having a phone…
not sounding like fun to you, is it!!
Do you hate us so much because we cared?
Have we not given enough of all that we’ve shared?
I’m at my wit’s end ~ I’m sure Grandpa looks down
with tears in his eyes and his mouth in a frown.
Sure wish I were with him and our Lord and Maker
Can’t wait ’til God says, “It’s now time to take her.”
If only we’d known what was in store for us then…
what a different future it might have been!

Grains of Sand

The ocean ~ wow, I'll not get over seeing it again
Each time for me is as the very first one
Its power, its strength ~ the force of the ocean
I liken the effect like a strong love potion
Standing in awe of its breadth and its splendor
Puts me in my place ~ as my stress I must render
Such a speck on this Earth are but we two
Like grains of this sand right under my shoe
We are but mere mortals as we live on this land
Here to love one another all that we can
This ocean is teeming with God's other creatures
We think we're so smart and have so many features
Not at all true in the eyes of our Savior
He loves everything and He shows no favor
I feel closer to God as I look out to sea
Knowing that He ~ is forever in me

Seeing the Truth

Oh, sometimes we think that we see ~ but not so
There are times when we wish to see it ~
Ain't gonna happen
Fooling only ourselves and no one else
Sooner or later, it hits us on the head like a hammer!
Yes, the truth ~ hard to take at times
We've all been there, many more times than
We'd like to admit.
And some, many more times than others.
We never really learn, do we?
Did we really know deep down in our hearts, but not listen
Or was it a gut feeling we had and brushed aside ~
Sticking our heads in the sand to hide.
It's sad that we do this to one another
Yet ~ it has always been this way
And will go on forever, I guess
Who gains from this?
I'll never know ~
Honestly!

A Wee Glass

It's the tartness, the coolness, the shavings of ice
the salt and the lime ~ they all make it taste nice
I don't take too much from the bottle you see
a wee glass now and then, when I'm not drinking tea

In the heat of the summer, when it's humid and hot
give me a beer, and I'll drink on the spot
When out with some friends, and it's time to dine
it'll be a fine bottle ~ red or white wine

Going back to my favorite, just Jose and myself
I open the fridge and take him from the shelf
The auto ice maker puts crushed ice in my glass
and with salt and the lime I make another pass

Two is my limit on a night all alone ~
enough to warm me right to the bone
I'm sleeping much better with Jose at my side
He's my best friend since my dear hubby died

And So I Start Anew

Here we go again ~ as hand takes up the pen
not knowing where it will lead
as it goes ~ I simply follow
somewhere deep within,
swirling thoughts and feelings converge
they swell in my heart ~ fall out onto paper
at times seeming to overtake all else
keeping me late into the night
I am at their mercy ~ but, I write

My Spirit

Another day to kiss good-bye
how wasteful I've become
It used to be that every morn
I was happy to see the sun

Not that I don't have good times
I have my family and my friends
There's just this emptiness inside
with which I must contend

One can't know my wish to change
and turn my life around
If only it were that easy
for my spirit to be found

It left me on a warm March day
as I was taken by surprise
As my dear husband of many years
died right before my eyes

They say that only time can heal
and God will help me through
But time seems to just stand still
and I don't know what to do

The Good Old Days

The ocean, the sun, the great salt air
Hot sand, cool drinks, gulls everywhere
Waves crashing, gentle breezes, and such
I've always loved the ocean so much
Airplanes dragging their banners behind
Tiny birds dancing as the waters rewind
Children digging with plastic shovels in hand
Mothers fighting a battle with all that sand
Sun bathers lathering up with odorous oil
Couples picking up shells as waves recoil
Fishermen casting for the biggest one
The surfers and divers having their fun
Loving seniors walking hand in hand
Remembering young days spent on this sand
Thinking that time would last always
~knowing now ~
those were the good old days

You Can Tell Me

Looking into eyes so blue ~ peering deep inside
what is it I see, what is it you hide
Is there pain, is there trouble
from years long ago
You can tell me ~ I really want to know
I think I see tears ~ old ones and new
are these tears for others ~
or are they for you
The pain that you suffer, is it from within
You can tell me ~ I know where you've been
Do I see doubt in there amidst all the rest
I hope it's not me you doubt ~
I am the best
That sadness I see, is it from today
You can tell me ~ I'll make it go away
I also see love down deep in that blue
Is that love for me ~ for me and for you
You can tell me for I know what to do
But wait just a moment ~ this is confusing
Is it me in this mirror
that I am using
All those tears, love, sadness and pain
I see them from outside ~
and you from within

The Spring

A tree grows barren with the season losing all its glory
So much the same goes on with her
I'll tell you of her story
Her time was many years ago ~
Spring was then the season
She budded in the sunlight ~
Blossomed without reason
She danced in tune
As gentle winds tossed her 'round about
Showing lovely petals ~
Fragrant without doubt
Oh so many did admire…
her beauty, style and stature
But there was only one ~
For her heart to capture
Together they grew through the years
So much to understand
How to make it through this life ~
Growing hand in hand
Now she's facing harsh times ~
Winter's unforgiving chill
She stands alone ~ so tired and worn
Waiting for God's will

More Than My Sister

She's so much more than a sister to me
always there when I need her to be

She's darling ~ she's funny
makes me laugh and makes me cry
We share a special closeness
we hate to say good-bye

She's so much more than a sister to me
my closest friend when I need her to be

She's giving ~ she's caring
makes me laugh and makes me cry
She has the soul of an angel
yet she has no wings to fly

She's so much more than a sister to me
so much between us that no one can see

She's sharing ~ and she shows intellect
knows what to say ~ just when to say it
She boosts me up when I feel like heck
there are no two sisters this close-knit

Having her for my sister ~ ever grateful I'll be
For there is no one else as special as she

Sunset

A flaming red-orange sun blazing against a dull, gray sky
lingers over the far-away tree tops
spreading its pinkish glow over the still waters
a day of darkness and mist ends in spectacular brilliance
telling of things to come

Our lives are much the same ~
periods of sadness and darkness
eventually giving way to happiness
filled with the laughter of lighter times

Times when the everyday sunset takes us by surprise
reminding us of the past
the present ~
and the future all at once
helping us bring things into perspective ~
reminding each
of our small part in this world
and how important we are to one another

This sunset reminds me of the greater picture
we all need things that bring us back ~
back to where we need to be

The Mist

the mist drifts softly by my window
taking on a life all its own
meandering through the trees
seeming ~ to surround my home
I see..
the breeze it travels on today
twisting....turning all around
in a slow, deliberate way
it's growing darker by the hour
mist glows by soft street light
as it turns to a rain shower
far sounds of a gull in flight
take me back to times gone by
walking on the shore ~
memories come flooding back
of one I have no more
treasured times of long ago
with one I loved dearly
these times never fade
he's in my mind so clearly
if only I could bring him back
just for one more kiss
to hold his hand ~ look in his eyes
walk with him in the mist

Stop the Snow

The snow softly floats from the sky to the ground
Nary a wind doth blow ~
As quiet as it can be, not a soul is around
Let it snow, let it snow, let it snow

The wondrous peaceful landscape belies
Just what's coming for all ~
As beauty blankets and covers the earth
And the snow continues to fall

Trees bow down all laden in white
reaching the ground with their limbs
Objects begin to disappear ~
Birdbaths are filled to their rims

As the winds pick up driving the snow
We huddle to gather for heat
We're all bundled up with no place to go
Except out to shovel the street

Now we've had quite enough of this white stuff
to do us 'til the end of all time
How much can we take, how many snowmen to make
Before it makes us just lose our minds

As pretty as it may be
I've seen enough for now ~
I'm going to throw this shovel away
Just bring on the snow plow

Rivers of Tears

I hear the distant drums sending messages across the land
Reaching from the mountains to the shoreline with its sand
These messages traveled just as fast as the ones we send today
Without computers or the web ~ arrived without delay

Life was much harder then, so dear for all to keep
Everything was treasured ~ in every soul so deep
If we'd take lessons to our hearts from the first American
We'd learn to live as the Red Man did ~ on this our precious land

The American Indian didn't rape this land we call our own
He treated it with respect and built on it his home
He took not from it more than his family may need
He always showed respect ~ never was there greed

I could never understand and still can't to this day
Where do we come off ~ taking everything away
We abuse and misuse this land we call our own
We have never really learned ~ what was already known

We will end up like the Indian toward the ending of our time
All shoved into one corner of this land that we call "mine"
We deserve no more than this ~ what goes around comes back
We need to learn respect and love ~ and not just think "attack"

The Spirits of the days gone by are looking over all ~
Must make amends for all we've done, on our knees must fall
Beg forgiveness from our God ~ and make changes in our ways
Respect this Earth and all it gives, this alone will save

I offer my apology for all the wrongs throughout the years
For all the pain and suffering and the rivers full of tears
I know it all continues for you, even as I write
My hope is for more to understand ~ and begin to see the light

Alone

As the last rays of sun settle low in the sky
I wonder of the night to come
Will it be long and lonely
as the ones before ~
or will I get a reprieve from this oneness
that has settled into my life
and into my heart ~
Am I doomed ~
doomed to this cold, bleak, and lonely existence
the world continues to flourish around me ~
in spite of me
Oh to be able to join in on that world~
that life ~
Yes, LIFE ~ not merely existence
Do I dare hope for this ~
it all seems so distant at this time
so far removed from where I have come to be
Totally ~
alone

Golden Spring

First buds of spring have all but gone
when God sends out his best
for in the April morn and dew these outshine the rest
her fragrance is unsurpassed by other bush or flower
the essence holds you in her spell
with its hypnotizing power
deep green leaves surround them all ~
almost a heart in shape
as if to show her love, her blooming cannot wait
the colors, oh, the colors ~ just takes one's breath away
some are dark, others more pale…
they change throughout the day
the lilac is the prize of spring,
it's worth its weight in gold
I shall never tire of them ~ such a beauty to behold

Angel Eggs

The land of little angels has finally come to be
a place where it all begins ~
for no one else to see
God creates these angel eggs ~
with a sprinkling on the flowers
a heart is placed in each
containing His own powers
as each angel hatches
from its little egg within
He sends each on its way
so the healing can begin
if you're asking for His help
please know it's on its way
for I thought I saw one leaving here
earlier today

A Tear Is Shed in Silence

to think of what may have been,
if we had been set free
to soar upon the breathless winds
to land wherever be
sinking into fertile earth
awaiting mountain's dew
sending forth our new growth ~
a sprout ~ and then a few
shooting up toward heaven
seeking rays of golden sun
growing stronger ~ ever taller
as each new day is done
our fate was not to be that
of the other seeds that flew
ours was to stay tethered here
and turn an autumn hue
a tear is shed in silence
as we linger here to die
this tear is felt by all ~
as life goes passing by

Woodland Lanterns

The sun shines dappled rays
Down along the wooded glen
As I meander 'round the thickets
I breathe the moist air in
Someone's leading me along this path
Calling me to come in ~
Bids me enter deeper…
To where I've never been
Oh ~ the beauty to behold
Delicate yellow flowers…
Suspended from red stems
Emitting magical powers
My way is now assured
By the Woodland Lantern's glow
As I delve even deeper ~
For all I wish to know

The Face of Death

Eyes of hollowness
deep with emptiness
sadness
a face so devoid of emotions
solitude
her son ~ taken from her in an instant
leaving behind only memories
and a child's love
this void ~ this abyss
unfathomable
by all…
unless
you've lost your child
she is torn apart
inside and out
struggling to heal physically ~
as she continues to delve deep within
her emotions
and
her mind

His Angel

Her hair is soft of golden brown
Sunlit streaks surround her crown.
She walks as if she floats on air ~
Her skin is pure and oh so fair.
Rosebud lips adorn her face,
Her dress entirely made of lace.
Sky blue eyes brighten her stare ~
She seems to roam without care.

Who could this mystery maiden be?
Has she come to talk with me?
I hear no words, but understand ~
As she takes me by my hand.
My trust in her is so complete,
I must kneel down by her feet.
A calmness overcomes my being ~
Now I know what I am seeing…

An angel sent from above,
She is full of eternal love.
My heart is right there in her hands ~
As she tells me of the plans.
All my sorrow she will take;
My tears will dry, my heart won't ache…
My memories will all remain ~
But no more suffering, no more pain.

How can this be, how is this done?
This could only come from One.
He died for us and our sins ~
He resides deep within.
One who feels all our sorrows,
One who knows our tomorrows.
He sent His angel just for me ~
To take away my misery.

Rag Doll

there is nothing more I can say
I am empty ~
drained of all emotions
the only feelings left
are those of a rag doll
all tattered and torn
thrown in a heap
no good anymore
to lay there and weep
so lonely and poor
no one notices me
just kick me aside
and let me be
and let me cry

The Book of Life

Leafing through my book of life ~ I like not what I see
for some things I have done and others I've let be ~

Nothing can change the past, of this I am so sure
all that I can surely do ~ is try to be more pure

Take things not for granted and go out of my way
to help all the others ~ in all I do and say

Spend time with the sick and love them all I can
give straight from my heart ~ as is in His plan

Gather all my strength and spread faith to mankind
don't live in the past ~ this won't help, you'll find

So, don't close your book up yet ~ you're not at the end
You must keep on writing 'til He comes for you, my friend

All By Herself

All by herself ~ no one at all ...
hours all alone
no one to call

With her family ~ how can this be ...
days all alone
no one to see

It's no wonder he caught her ~ in her time of need ~
he was there
to fill her need

Says he's there for her, but she knows more...
this is for him
she has opened the door

He stuck his foot in, she's a little afraid
should she continue
plans already made

Or go where she belongs
back on the shelf,
no one to call
All by herself

Your Tears

(dedicated to my daughter, Robin)

Your tears are felt not just by you
They touch my cheek ~ I feel them, too
They trickle down into my heart
Forever broken ~ from the start

I may not help them go away
For they will be there every day
It's all a part of where we've been
It all comes from loving him

When one cries sorrow in the night
She's not alone in her plight
Her mother's there…if not to touch
Please know she loves you very much

We share these tears as we did him
A gift from heaven now held within
There is never a gift more precious
Than thy child…Lord, Please Bless Us

Pondering

There is a space, comes at high tide
In this place that I can hide.
To be alone, then bring me back…
My thoughts atone to where I'm at.
To stay away, my soul to rest,
Another day put to the test.
I hunger for the test of time,
When nevermore is ever mine.

Sweet Sleep

Oh, sweet sleep,
tuck me in ~ take me away…
drain my body of sin
where I've gone astray
relax me within ~
take troubles and stress
fill me with love
and tenderness

So when I wake up
to the new day…
I'll be able to take on
the work and the play
To greet you again
tomorrow's eve ~
and ask you to take me
again with you please

Butterfly Milk

In the heart of every flower
~ all the flowers ever grown
there lies a special place
to us it is unknown

Only the graceful butterfly
knows of this magic heart
It's where the drop of milk is left
before he's to depart

Just one drop of Butterfly Milk
deposited in this heart
gives the flowers dewy colors
and fragrance from the start

So, next time you see a butterfly
resting on a flower…
think of this magic potion
giving all its power

Dream Spiral

The beauty of the Spiral are the angels there inside
wrapped up in frothy colors…
trying so to hide
You seem to think the dreams you dream
come from deep within ~
I beg to differ with you…
for I know where they've been
These lovely angels from afar
are gathering…dream dust
They come together in this Spiral
to sprinkle down on us ~
If you're among the chosen ones
and the dream dust graces you
you'll dream a dream of love…
the one who loves you true

Morning Mist

Ripples on the water ~
seem to stir
the morning mist
Trees rising in the
distance…
as the lake
by sun is kissed
The sun creeps
ever higher
bringing
colors into view
as morning mist
is softly flowing…
dancing
with the dew

Voices

I've listened to the voices
hidden deep inside my head
I've tried to ignore them,
yet heard every word they've said
They lead me to places
where I ought not to be
Struggling within me ~
trying not to see

One said to me, "Go ahead,
he just might be the one."
I heard the voice and ran with it,
to find my honey bun.
Oh, he was sweet alright ~
just what I was looking for.
I jumped in with both feet
and closed and locked the door.

I heard a voice again say,
"Go ahead and have some fun."
I got so tied up with this guy
yes ~ he was to be the one…
Now I hear the voices laughing ~
I hear them loud and clear,
"How could she be so stupid
to think he'd hold her dear."

I try to stop these voices
lurking deep inside…
for they continue laughing ~
while I feel like I have died
Will I never learn my lesson
will age not help me by
I must continue on alone…
as the voices hear me cry

The Barn

far across the meadow
guarded by trees…
trees beginning to accept
the hues of autumn
morning awakens
to a blanket of frost…
the first frost ~
it's an omen
of winter's unforgiving chill
to come
oblivious to the seasons,
standing in nature's den
nestled there…
in comfort is
the barn

Days Go By

leave not a stone
left unturned
search for all
you have yearned
as days go by ~
time won't stand still
you can't retrieve
what's over the hill
one day you'll wake up
old like me…
wondering ~
how it came to be
the last days
you'll ever see
before you know
you just won't be

Darkness Invades

The sun pulls over its cover of darkness
as it slowly sinks into the lavender-filled sky
mirrored…
in the peaceful, ever-darkening lake.
The surrounding forest fades
from green to black.
Echoes of trees
forever etched against
the backdrop of the heavens,
stand stark and tall
reflecting their stature
on placid waters.
As darkness invades,
sun still abides…
lighting the earth in patches
of brilliant hues
seeking to tease our memories
for what is to come…
tomorrow

Colors

As I stand here to paint with palette in hand,
I look at the colors trying to understand...
the picture of life that was painted by me;
am I really happy ~ with all that I see?

My childhood was brushed in purple hues.
There was verbal, mental and sexual abuse;
drinking, divorce, and government food,
and Mom alone trying to raise the brood.

All the places we lived were colored dark red.
We were always moving and sharing a bed;
not having nice clothes or even a bike,
wanting to be as the others ~ all alike.

My teen years were painted a lovely pink.
I came out of my shell and started to think...
I was just as good as all of the others,
guys were cool ~ I never had any brothers.

Adulthood for me shined a sunny yellow.
I met and married my favorite fellow;
many good times ~ for better or worse,
we lived our lives, no time to rehearse.

In mid-life ~ the brush strokes turned to blue.
I lost the one ~ I loved so true.

My life forever changed on that day,
emptiness, sorrow seem here to stay.

This takes me to where I am at this time.
as I stare at my palette and try to find…
a color to paint these last few years
as the colors begin to mix with my tears.

The Pond of Blurred Emotions

I am the pond of blurred emotions
where all my feelings
there combine
They flow so freely
as they shouldn't…
being tangled in the lily vine
The swirling waters
lend no hand ~
keep me all stirred up
inside
Going too deep..
only to surface
Ripples ~ my outgoing tide
How I'd love
to travel time…
Return to life
before
the pond
Emotions on
an even keel ~
To live my life
and go
beyond

Joseph

He's a quiet young man
Of fourteen ~
Spending a little vacation time
With Grandma
So polite and helpful
And growing up so quickly ~
Yet has the face of a child
And an honest heart
Made of gold
Today ~ he is doing some jobs
For me
Things his Grandpa used to do
Since Grandpa's passing ~
Things seem to pile up undone
Joey's offer to help
Is welcomed
We've spent time at the pool
Running errands, shopping,
Visiting family, playing,
Laughing and loving
It's such a pleasure
To enjoy one of my
Grandchildren
All to myself
Alone

Summer Storms

Rolling thunder
Softly rattles my windows..
As the beating rain drops
Make the awnings roar
Green awnings ~
That whip with each gust of wind
Snapping sharply..
Then fluttering lightly
As rain pours from them
I find if I stay
In the corner near the railing
Surrounding the stairs..
I can witness all this
And still be dry
Oh, an occasional spray
Cools my hot skin
And every once in a while
A lightening bolt
Jolts my mind
Back
To reality
I love the rain ~
The thunder
The lightening…
It's refreshing, soothing
~ invigorating
All at the same time

Shades of Green

As I look across my yard
at all the things there growing
I think that I can't count
the shades of green there showing
The trees so stately as they stand
leaves a flutter in the breeze
Show different hues of green
an artist's brush to tease
Not one could capture all this beauty
we're given free of charge
Only God Himself could create
a palette quite this large

Special Friends

You know you are a special friend
We share secrets ~ me and you
Yet we go on about our lives
Doing what we must do

I hold you in a special place
Right inside my heart…
Not everybody goes in there
But you did from the start

If you ever need to talk to me
Know I'll be here just for you
Send me a little email ~
And I'll get right back to you

The Lady in the Chair

As I peer in through my window,
I see someone sitting there.
She appears to be reading
While sitting in my chair.

I cannot see her face,
But her hair is silver gray.
She's sort of bent over
In an elderly kind of way.

Her hands are very shaky
Turning the pages of her book.
She takes a magnifying glass
To have a better look.

My heart softens for her…
She's as peaceful as can be,
As she turns I see her wrinkles
And I realize ~ it's me.

Photo of a Bird

Appearing statuesque
In a stream so pure and cool
Nature's canvas as a backdrop
His reflection in this pool
Searching for a morsel
To soothe his appetite
Feathers ever soft
In varying shades of white
He eyes my approach to him
But ~ moves not away
My camera keeps on clicking
Yet he prefers to stay
Such a beauty to behold
A creature of this land
Always part of nature
Made by God's own hand

A Million Tears

They're never ending
These many tears
As I think back
Reviewing the years
Scrapes and cuts
And darkness fears
Caused lots of crying
With little tears
Then first loves
Ones forevermore
All left my tears
Puddled on the floor
The wedding day
Joy-filled tears
A baby born
Years of tears
Some of joy
Others sorrows
Filled my heart
For all tomorrows
Tears of death
Pour from my heart
Never ending
Since their start
Combining now with
Longing tears
Which now fill

These lonely years
When adding up
All these years
I must have cried
A million tears

The Soup Kitchen

Ladies all busy with all the food
Gents setting up tables and chairs
Kids helping, doing their bit
Setting on the table wares

The food is cooking and so is the help
Must be the hottest day of the year
The fans are blowing a gentle breeze
As the less fortunate start to near

They arrive in droves and tear at my heart
As I remember that saying of old
But for the Grace of God go I
As to my heart my hand I hold

The serving begins to feed hungry mouths
The old, the young, and the teens
While all the time my mind gives thanks
For all that I have and my means

They have no shame for it's not up to them
Can't change their lots in life
To live in the streets ~ no house to keep
To continually live in strife

As we clean up the kitchen and go on our way
We leave with a different heart
Just one day here serving the poor
Gives each day a better start

Her Turn

The woman within, cries out…in pain
To all who hear…but yet, in vain
She's as a star in a clouded sky
Far out of sight,
Yet wonders why her light still shines…
But from within
Outside
All is dim
This star…not long to burn
She's seen love ~ She had her turn

Water's Edge

I arrived at high tide ~ a beautiful time
All the ugliness hidden
Fog and mist still drifting over the water
I sat down upon the only step on the dock
Leaning up against the piling
Breathing in the salty air
Listening to the water lapping against the wood
The water, so close ~ it splashes up
Through the planks at the slightest wake
It's a holiday and boating traffic is brisk
I can still lose myself here
Sun is burning off the fogginess
I liked it better with the fog
I walk on down through the still damp path
Hidden in the shade of trees and grasses
Staying shy of the poison ivy ~
Finding a lonely, shaded fishing pier
Ah ~ yes, as I sit next to the swaying grasses
Tucked away in the greenery
Oblivious to boaters passing by
I close my eyes and listen to the sounds
An electric motor purring along behind a jon boat
The soft rumble of an inboard pushing a yacht
Laughter and the splashing of two boys in kayaks
It's much like a parade ~
Off in the distance, beyond my sight from shore
And only because it's caught by the sunlight

I see a line zing out into the water
It then disappears from where it came
It's hot now as the sun has taken over
I continue my walk,
Wishing only that I had started earlier
I'll return later ~ in the rain ~ if I'm lucky
Leaving my troubles at the water's edge
I head back home

My Laughter

So Long, Sucker!

All this traffic is just killing me
I'm not an aggressive person, you see.
Day after day as I fight for a lane
this darn driving just gets me insane

Do you ever wonder while driving to work,
right along side of a stupid jerk,
"Does this guy really belong to someone?
Who in the world would call HIM hon!"

The thruways are full of aggressive creeps,
We know they got horns ~ we hear all the beeps.
They give you the finger, then yell for a while,
I just give them a wave ~ and flash them a smile.

This just seems to make their tempers rise
The roads are just full of these bully guys.
I wave and then leave them behind in my dust
As I cruise on by ~ in my bucket of rust

My New Neighbor

To keep in touch, computers are great~
You can IM or e-mail, no matter how late
But the sound of your voice just warms my heart
And stirs my senses right from the start.

You sound like you're right next door to me
What a well-beaten path THAT would be!
We could meet at your place and make love in the bath
And then at my place, what fun we would have

I'd come for some sugar ~ you'd come for some tea
We'd keep the neighbors busy trying to see
We could nap on my deck, skinny dip in your pool
You could chase after me and I after you!

We'd be the talk of J-towne, I'd bet money on that
We must try to take more miles off that map.
But for now we will settle for our occasional meetings
And be thankful and stick with the online greetings

The Teens

I have two teens ~ what a different breed
They're always eating ~ they need to feed
Of things they eat? Well, there's not a lot
It's pizza, or Steakums, or tator tots
Maybe burgers or dogs ~ or why not eat out!
They stay up late ~ sleep in, and then they shout
Always tired and with NOTHING to do
Oh, how I wish that I were you
The clothes that they wear just don't fit right
No room in the bathroom, they always must fight
Who goes in first and who has to be last
Must not take long ~ Got to be fast
The phone is in use for hour after hour
The milk is left out on the counter to sour
The reptile is gone, the fish are not fed
Please don't let that lizard be under MY bed
The floor is all covered in clothes for a rug
I'm hoping ~ that I'll not find a bug
There are marks on the floor and holes in the wall
Not one seems to know how they got there at all
But then I thank God for these kids every day
They're how my hair got totally gray
They keep me going ~ even though in a haze
Thank God school starts in just a few days

Poor Tech Man

Boy, do I need help with this darn computer
I think I'd do better with rotor-rooter
Had to call MSN and talk to the tech man
He said he was the man ~ with the plan
After playing 20 questions ~ he knew what he had
"It was an old lady and this would be BAD"
Unaware of the "version," and ~ "I have a browser?"
"Do you really want me to push that button now, sir?"

The longer we talked, seemed the dumber I got
This man had patience ~ I'd say a lot!
NOW, I know not to push backspace if it's highlighted
When things disappeared, I really got excited
He talked me through searches and changes I made
So good of him to help me and not to get paid
I got a new password ~ Oh no, not again!
Having trouble with those and also my PIN

Poor man had to leave me ~ so he bid me farewell
I begged him to stay ~ this was going to be hell!
As I have but one phone line we had to let go
"Please don't leave me now, John, I don't know if I know"
I'll call back tomorrow ~ as it's STILL not working
Somewhere in there a bug must be lurking
I have a ticket number to give this NEW man
This will be NUMBER 5 ~ he'll help if he can

Room to Roam

It ain't easy getting old
I'm at a cross road in my life
Must get a smaller home ~
'cause I'm no longer a wife

My hubby died five years ago
I don't need all this space
No one to paint and fix it up
Can't let it go to waste

Could mean an apartment
or maybe just a condo ~
But then there is a rancher,
I'd better check my escrow

My son came up with an idea
Why not come with them
An in-law apartment
They'd have it built right in

So we all piled in the Windstar
My son, his wife and me ~
They have a thirteen-year-old
and also one who's three

We drove around and took a look
at just what's on the market

To tell the truth, I've changed my mind,
almost told them to park it

If you've spent three hours in a van
with kids, and food and toys
It's like you really don't need to
move in with all that noise

How to tell them "thanks, but no thanks"
I've decided to stay at home
I love this big old house so much
It gives me room to roam.

Nicholas

Nick is such a charming child,
full of love and laughter.
He greeted me with a homemade basket
he was looking after.
It held a bunch of jellybeans in colors of the rainbow.
They lay on green Easter grass,
"It really doesn't grow."
He sat right down, asking me which color was my favorite ~
I chose blue; none were there,
so a red one,
~ he would get it
His little hand reached right in and grabbed it up with glee
I popped it in my mouth ~
as I thanked him joyfully.
Then came the parting of the beans
and all that straggly grass,
which revealed some silver change
and quite a bit of cash!
He pondered for a moment ~ as if thinking pensively
"I think the red ones are one dollar
just for you from me."
"One dollar for a jelly bean?" I asked,
"Isn't that quite high?"
"Oh no," was his answer, "and I'll tell you why,
The number one is the lowest number ~
the LOWEST of them all!"
I was dealing with a businessman
~~ who's only 3 feet tall ~~

The Gold Camp Floozy

They'd pan for gold from morning 'til night
What a sweaty crew they'd be
She'd watch over them ~ there'd be nary a fight
The Gold Camp floozy was she

She had her eyes set on a lone wolf named Jess
As she planned to take him to bed
She'd wink and she'd smile and give him a tease
Throwing that boa back over her head

Jess was tired ~ when in the moonlight
The floozy appeared by his side
All I know is that the feathers were flyin'
And he got one hell of a ride

The lone wolf named Jess thought it but a dream
As Grandfather sun smiled down
'til he saw the brightness of colored feathers
Strewn all about on the ground

The Drink

As I tipped my glass up and finished the drink
I looked through the bottom and started to think
This is what I might see if I drink many more
And I'll probably end up right on the floor

I'm not taken to drinking too much by myself
Days go by when it stays on the shelf
But now and again ~ when I feel the ache
I'll get it down and a few I will take

It warms up my innards right down to my toes
Makes me relax forgetting my woes
Changes my mood to good from bad
Makes me forget what a day I've had

If I have a friend who'll imbibe with me, too
Oh, what a wonderful thing this will do
We get happy together discussing the crap
Ridding ourselves of this and of that

Most drinking buddies go way back in time
Remembering drafts you could buy for a dime
To hell and back ~ that's where they've been
And I bet you a beer they'll go there again

Man

Is it possible at all to describe this being called Man
I think no matter how I try ~ I don't think I can
At first they seem so down to earth,
honest and sincere
Then something happens after this
that strikes my heart with fear
I want to believe all Man speaks,
his writings and his actions
But then his stories begin to change ~
something starts to happen
If they would only speak the truth ~
they'd have nothing to recall
Wouldn't this be easier on everyone after all
Is it built right into Man to forget all special days?
Yet he remembers football and all the tricky plays.
Does Man know your favorite color,
your favorite of them all?
He can't forget the colors
of the teams who throw that ball!
Is Man sitting in that SUV leaning on the horn ~
Waiting for you to dress the kids
and bring out the newborn
Who in the world does he think he is,
sitting there in shades
Yeah, he's cool alright ~ probably thinking of barmaids
When you're sick and don't feel good ~
you go on about your work

Unlike Man who stays in bed and moans ~
Gee, he's such a jerk!
So I rest my case and to this day I still can't understand
Why we were put here on earth with this thing called Man

One Ringy Dingy

You've reached my number,
Listen up, I'll tell you what to do
If you'd like to leave a message for me ~
Press the # 2
If you'd like to make an appointment at a future time
Then you can go ahead and…
Press the # 9
I feel I must be truthful and tell you even more
If you're a telemarketer ~
Try pressing # 4
This will get you nowhere, but you won't be late
If this is my lover, mmmmm,
Please press # 8
If you're calling to collect money, what we have is none
In that case only ~
Please press # 1
If this is a true emergency ~
Press the # 7
These calls aren't taken anymore,
I send them straight to Heaven
If you're a long-lost relative ~ and think I'm still alive
You can go ahead and
Press the # 5
If you dialed me in error because you just can't see
Why not put your glasses on and
Press the # 3
And if you're feeling lucky ~
Press the # 6
This will let you listen to all my limericks

Don't Fall Asleep at the Pool

Reclining at pool side ~ the sun shining down
All lathered with oil
Wearing a hat for my crown

I feel like a queen ~ awaiting her maiden
as she brings forth
her basket so laden

This basket is brimming right to the handle
with sexy things
that may cause a scandal

There's a tiny bikini with little strings
and big dark glasses
among other things

As I rummage through this basket of tricks
my eyes light on something
and I am transfixed

It's so soft, so rubbery ~ so good to the touch
I just want to hold and
play with it so much

I try to hide it from the gang at the pool
for this is so great ~
it's waaaaay too cool

It's out of the chaise ~ to the water I flee
holding it ever
so close to me

I feel myself drowning…and as I wake up
I see I'm still clutching
my little rubber duck

Country Music Radio

Don't look in my window…don't listen at my door
Someone's telling stories that I've heard before
My radio plays songs for all the world to hear
containing all my memories, some I hold so dear
All the words I hear…and every song they play
come straight from my heart,
like it happened yesterday
Sweet words of surrender…
Love that's gone astray ~
Married men and losers
or one living far away
You all know my feelings hidden deep inside of me
Go ahead and sing it loud wherever you may be
I'll just sing along ~ the words I know so true
For each and every day,
I create more for you

One More Drink

Some days it ain't worth gettin' outta bed
Should have just rolled over and covered my head
Everything's in a mess ~ Everyone's in a stink
I guess I'll just have...one more drink

The mail was delivered ~ but the check wasn't there
Phoned up the bank, but the gal didn't care
She called the main office to see what they think
I'll wait for her call and have...one more drink

The washer's disconnected ~ due to the work crew
They jackhammered all day, I wish they were through
The water's all over, they've taken out the sink
It's a damned awful mess, I need...one more drink

My Internet friend has a bug up his a$$
It seems as though I have not enough class
Some days he drives me right to the brink
This is one reason why I need...one more drink

Island Liquors ~ it's such a wonderful place
They know me well by the smile on my face
My goods are all packaged and they give me a wink
Now I can go home and have...one more drink

Is there a moral to this story ~ this story of olde
It may be "Don't drink and go out in the cold"
But seeing it's summer and I'm so in the pink
It won't hurt me to have just...one more drink

My Cyber Catch

So many men ~ So little time
I search and search hoping to find
That special one who's "Oh, So Right"
Hoping he'll show up on my screen tonight

I've started a filing system now ~
I guess you're wondering just how...
Well, there's the "too young" file,
What do they want?
They use fancy names and real cute font

Another file is named "no ed"
These are the ones with no brain in their head
Then there's the file of "dirty talkers"
This one's full and they're probably stalkers

I have a file called ~ "what was I thinking"
When I emailed these I must have been drinking
We move right along to ~ "alrighty then"
These guys sound like really great men
Just one little thing they forgot to mention
Is the wife at home who gives no attention

So many files ~ So little time
I'll run out of space before I find ~
My lover boy, my perfect match
The one for me ~ *'My Cyber Catch'*

Good Neighbor Larry

We have a neighbor ~ who lives right next door
He's so kind and gentle ~ and never a bore
He has been so helpful over all these years
We have shared good times…and also the tears

No one could ask for a better neighbor and friend
For he's good to all ~ no need to pretend
We've borrowed things and he has fixed my "john"
He's cooked my burgers and worked on my pond

He has come when called to chase a burglar away
He tackled a big snake that held us at bay
He's lectured my kids on the don'ts and the dos
Especially when they snuck in the window at 2 (a.m.)

I'll probably have to let up on him a bit
'Cause I heard something ~ just can't believe it
It's something about him that I think is so nifty
I heard the "Old Man" is turning FIFTY!!

HAPPY BIRTHDAY, LARRY

Just What Was I Thinking

Take it from me and you will see
There's one thing that should never be done
Don't color your hair on Margarita Day
Even though it sounds like fun

Why, it was just a couple days ago
When I combined the two ~
Really not a good idea
For now I have a "new do"

The first few steps went well
It was all down hill from there
When time came to put the streaks in
They went just everywhere

As if that's not enough
It seems I mixed the concoction wrong
I was so busy drinking Margaritas
And singing my favorite song

Where the color used to be blonde
It's now a chestnut hue…
Then there's another strange color
Why, it looks almost like a blue

I'll tell you one thing for sure
Margaritas and hair color don't mix
For here I sit ~ my hair's screwed up
And I think I'm going to be sick!

I'll Be Good

From now on ~ I'll be a good girl
I'll do my very best
I'll mind my "Ps & Qs"
I will pass that test
Don't worry about me
My eyes will no more flirt
I'll not look at the fellows
My heart will never hurt

For I'm a grandmother ~ you see
I'm aging ~ getting old
I should be in that rocker
Recalling stories told
Instead, I have my shorts on
Plus my hot pink top
To hell with what my kids say
I think I'll never stop

First there is the mailman
So cute in shorts & socks
He always puts his mail
Right inside my box
Next I see my neighbor
Soon he will be fifty
I'll be at his party
This will be so nifty

Of course there is the lifeguard
Over at the pool
He is so tan and tall
He just makes me drool
Don't mention this to anyone
Not my kids or grandkids please
Don't even tell my great granddaughter
That her great grandma's still a tease

Home Repairs

Will this construction never end
I'm an old lady ~ how much can I take
They wear those sexy blue jeans
My heart will have a quake

Oh, then there are the tool belts
Slung low upon their hips
That tugs the jeans down lower
Where I can see their slits

I really try to turn my eyes
Away from all such sights
For a woman at my age
I find this such a fright

It seems to be a day or two
Before it all will end
I'm wondering what else needs done
For which they must bend

I find this so disgusting ~
They're sweaty, hot and dirty
OH, they must have water
I'll get drinks ~ I'll not be flirty

For these guys are much younger
Way too young you see
I wonder what else needs fixing
Around this house for me

For Love or Money

Sit back,
Close your eyes,
Let me run my fingers through your hair
I'll massage your tired neck
Squeeze you here and there

Let's take this shirt off
'Tis the end of day
You'll not need it anymore
I'll rub your aching muscles
Right where they are sore

Stretch out here
On the chaise, honey
Your pants you'll not need either
Let me take them for you
For you need a little breather

Mmmmmm, you're looking good to me
Have a glass of chilled white zin
It'll help you to relax a bit
Get you ready
For the mood I'm in

Now that you're all relaxed
Stretched out there
Looking fine

Could you help me
Balance this checkbook
It seems I'm off a dime!

Sunglasses

I like to put my sunglasses on
they make things look so cool
the color is not brown or blue
but they have a pinkish hue

I especially like watching people
when they think I'm sound asleep
I always wear them at the pool ~
so at swimmers I can peep

Saw a guy take a dive in a Speedo,
thought it was really quite scary
he didn't know his gut was so big
& his backside was so darned hairy

The bikini clad gal was another ~
her lover's hands were so busy
I looked away, I just couldn't say…
but he had her in a real tizzy

Now at times I check out the lifeguard,
just for safety's sake ~ you know
Don't want him to burn, only to tan,
and don't let those tan lines show

As I slowly look around the pool ~
I'm always trying to see
who might be wearing glasses, too
and be looking back at me

Mustang Sally

I'm at the pool soaking up some rays
Remembering the happenings of yesterday
My first biker party ~ my head still aches
And at my age, for heaven's sake!

Billy the biker latched right on to me
I thought he was the "welcoming committee" you see
Long, curly, gray hair, cutoffs and bare feet
He was all too happy and ready to greet

As I sit here sipping white zin at the pool
I'm thinking I must have been quite the fool
The Karaoke machine was the beginning of the end
By then Billy and I had become good friends

The music was blaring and with a mic in my hand
We began to sing along with the band
I became "Mustang Sally" ~ as we really "got down"
Hips gyrating as Billy howled to the ground

The words became useless on the screen before me
By then I couldn't read and could barely see
We belted it out from days long ago
Billy was good ~ I was just "so-so"

The cameras came out and started to flash
Sally and Billy were the hit of the Bash
I bid my farewell after fight # 2
Alas ~ Mustang Sally rode off in the blue

The Widows' Ball

My one, my only, my love, my all…
Come with me to the Widows' Ball
I'll dance around the room with you
I'll wear my dress of powder blue

White ribbons tied up in my hair…
All the gents will turn and stare
All will see my love for you
That love shines in my eyes of blue

As I gaze at your handsome face…
You're toying with my strap of lace
You steer my dance steps toward a door
As we continue across the floor

This door leads to another room…
Where the janitor keeps the broom
We close the door and lock it tight
Darkness slowly becomes dim light

Our clothes fall quickly to the floor…
You push me up against the door
Passion takes the upper hand
We're dancing to a different band

No sooner said than we are done…
We grab our clothes and have to run

Straighten my hair ~ put on your tie
Don't forget to zip your fly

We'll try to ease ourselves back in…
Right where we should have been
Again we're dancing cheek to cheek
My heart still racing ~ legs still weak

My very first ever Widows' Ball…
I think I'll be attending all
For every time I sweep the floor
I'll remember our time behind that door

The Dance

The sax music plays in the background, as she slowly dances with him
He's breathing on her neck...the lights are way down dim

Their bodies sway with the music ~ in dreams of sweet surrender
He breathes her perfume in...his thoughts begin to wander

His hands play with her zipper, her scarlet dress falls to the floor
She steps right out of it...as they dance on some more

Her silken slip now joins her dress, she stands before him in her undies
He can't recall a dance like this ~ not in a month of Sundays

Her stockings and red heels...are more than he can take
He guides her to the bar ~ where sweet love they make

Now I've heard of "belly up to the bar, boys,"
but this isn't quite the same
And this really didn't happen...Honest!
Do you think that I'm insane!!